2/09

HOW A LAW IS PASSED

THE U.S. GOVERNMENT
HOW IT WORKS

★ ★ ★

THE U.S. GOVERNMENT
HOW IT WORKS

HOW A LAW
IS PASSED

BILL SCHEPPLER

CHELSEA HOUSE
PUBLISHERS
An imprint of Infobase Publishing

How a Law Is Passed

Copyright © 2007 by Infobase Publishing

All rights reserved. No part of this book may be reproduced or utilized in any form or by any means, electronic or mechanical, including photocopying, recording, or by any information storage or retrieval systems, without permission in writing from the publisher. For information, contact:

Chelsea House
An imprint of Infobase Publishing
132 West 31st Street
New York NY 10001

Library of Congress Cataloging-in-Publication Data
Scheppler, Bill.
  How a law is passed / Bill Scheppler.
     p. cm. — (The U.S. government: how it works)
  Includes bibliographical references and index.
  ISBN-13: 978-0-7910-9466-2 (hardcover)
  ISBN-10: 0-7910-9466-9 (hardcover)
  1. Legislation—United States.   2. Legislative bodies—United
States.   I. Title.   II. Series.

  KF4945.S34 2007
  328.73'0775—dc22   2006039236

Chelsea House books are available at special discounts when purchased in bulk quantities for businesses, associations, institutions, or sales promotions. Please call our Special Sales Department in New York at (212) 967-8800 or (800) 322-8755.

You can find Chelsea House on the World Wide Web at
http://www.chelseahouse.com

Text design by James Scotto-Lavino
Cover design by Ben Peterson

Printed in the United States of America
Bang NMSG 10 9 8 7 6 5 4 3 2 1

This book is printed on acid-free paper.

All links and Web addresses were checked and verified to be correct at the time of publication. Because of the dynamic nature of the Web, some addresses and links may have changed since publication and may no longer be valid.

CONTENTS

1

"THERE OUGHTA BE A LAW"

There ought to be a law requiring a new section of the Internet for kids only—like the children's areas they have in libraries! The only information, pictures, and media available would be kid friendly, and people who know what kids like would pack the section with new stuff. Any content for adults would be banned, and if it showed up, someone would remove it. Finally, if there were ways to chat with other kids or post comments and photos on a site, someone would keep an eye on that, too, and kick out any grown-ups.

Guess what? That law exists. In 2002, President George W. Bush signed into law the Dot Kids Implementation and Efficiency Act. This law requires a government

President George W. Bush (sitting) signed into law new legislation creating the kid-safe "Dot Kids" Internet domain on December 4, 2002. The domain is intended to contain only material that is appropriate for children under 13.

organization called the National Telecommunications and Information Administration (NTIA), part of the U.S. Department of Commerce, to create a special Internet subdomain dedicated to kids that only features content safe for children under 13 years of age. In addition to building the section, the NTIA is responsible for defining kid-friendly standards, creating a process for monitoring the content and interaction on the site, and resolving standards violations by immediately deleting content and banning users. NTIA launched Kids .us (www.kids.us) in September 2003.

How did the Dot Kids Implementation and Efficiency Act become law? On March 4, 2002, Representative John Shimkus introduced bill H.R.3833 to the House of Representatives. The bill was referred to the House Committee on Energy and Commerce, which subsequently referred it to the subcommittee on Telecommunications and the Internet. The committee reported the bill on May 8, and the House voted to pass it on May 21. On May 22, the Senate received the approved bill and referred it to the Committee on Commerce, Science, and Transportation, which in turn referred it to the subcommittee on Science, Technology, and Space. The committee recommended the act to the Senate on November 13, and the Senate passed the legislation the same day with one amendment. The House approved the Senate amendment on November 15 and presented the act to the president on November 26. On December 4, 2002, the president signed H.R.3833, enacting it as Public Law 107-317.

This is a quick overview of how one law was passed in the United States government. It is a process that is easy to grasp on the surface but becomes more complex as you learn about the legislature and the wide variety (not to mention high volume) of bills introduced to Congress each year. This book takes you step by step along a bill's path to becoming law and introduces you to all the participants who play a role in the process. So, the next time you have an idea that "oughta be a law," you will know how to take the first step.

2

How Congress Is Organized

The United States federal government is made up of three unique branches: executive, legislative, and judicial. Working together, the three branches form a powerful system for evolving our country's laws to meet new challenges while upholding the rights and responsibilities guaranteed by the U.S. Constitution. Working independently, no single branch is stronger than the other two, which ensures a balance of power and renders all three equally important. The legislative branch of the U.S. federal government is called Congress. This is the branch responsible for introducing and preparing legislation that may become new law.

As established by Article I of the Constitution, Congress is divided into two distinct yet complimentary parts: the House of Representatives, in which each member represents a relatively equal number of citizens; and the Senate, where delegates represent the entire state from which they are elected. Each body of Congress appoints its own leaders and functions by its own rules, but both play very similar roles in passing new legislation. The House and the Senate are further divided into committees, which provide expert focus on specific issues of proposed legislation prior to communicating to the entire Congress. This chapter provides an introduction to these key roles in the legislative process.

THE HOUSE OF REPRESENTATIVES

Truly the cornerstone of our democracy, the House of Representatives provides equal representation in Congress for every citizen of the United States, regardless of sex, race, economic status, or state of residence. The House of Representatives is made up of 435 members, each of whom represents an area of the country called a congressional district. The residents of a district choose the person they want to represent them in the House of Representatives by participating in general elections every two years. Once elected to Congress, representatives are the voices of their district residents, known as constituents, in the lawmaking process.

Every 10 years, the United States conducts a census to count its citizens. State governments then use population data generated by the census to redefine congressional

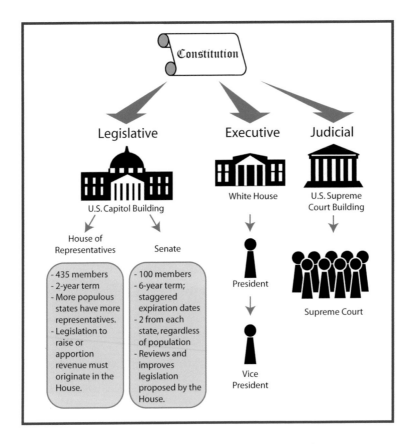

The chart above shows the different branches of government, including the legislative, executive, and judicial. Each of the three branches plays a specific role in the creation and maintenance of laws in the United States.

districts, ensuring that each member represents a similar number of constituents. As a result, more populous states have more representatives in Congress. California, for example, has 53 districts based on 2000 census data of 33.8 million residents, whereas Idaho, with 1.2 million, has just 2 districts. Although a greater number of representatives does not necessarily translate to greater power for a state, crafty governors can redraw district boundaries to gain presence for their political parties in Congress.

General elections occur on the first Tuesday after the first Monday in November during even-numbered years. On January 3 of the following year, the members of the House of Representatives convene in Washington, D.C., to begin the new congressional term. At the opening of a new term, representatives elect their House leader, known as the Speaker. The Speaker of the House is an incredibly powerful role because it influences many of the House committee assignments and determines the order in which the House addresses new legislation. The Speaker typically belongs to the House majority political party and often prioritizes legislation supported by the majority party over legislation endorsed by the minority. When they are in the same party, the Speaker of the House is the president of the United States' closest ally in all of Congress. When they are not, the Speaker can be the president's greatest political foe.

A term is divided into two year-long sessions. The chief function of Congress is to propose and pass legislation. The Constitution distinguishes the House from the Senate in this function, stating that only the House may propose legislation for raising and apportioning revenue. This refers to laws that increase taxes and laws that determine how the government spends its money.

Through the House of Representatives, ordinary citizens can make a significant impact on the lawmaking

The Capitol building in Washington, D.C., holds both houses of the U.S. Congress: the Senate and the House of Representatives. Each body has its own chamber, where all official business is conducted.

process. Because of the biennial election cycle, representatives are under constant review. They need to know that their constituents approve of the job they are doing, so they welcome feedback. This provides interested citizens with an opportunity to communicate their thoughts and concerns to someone who actually votes on federal legislation in Washington every day. Equally important is the ultimate tool of democracy—constituents have the power to vote one representative out of office in favor of another candidate who better represents their point of view.

THE SENATE

The second body of Congress is called the Senate. Its primary role in the lawmaking process is to review and improve legislation introduced by the House of Representatives. Representatives typically support legislation that addresses the immediate concerns of their constituents. Senators, who serve longer terms and in most cases represent larger constituencies, often amend House-approved legislation to ensure it is applicable to the broader public and will remain relevant over time. This system of checks and balances places the needs of the American people at the foundation of new legislation and at the same time leverages a long-term perspective to create better laws.

Article I, Section 3, of the Constitution specifies that each state elect two members to the Senate, which provides each state with equal representation, regardless of population. In 1959, Hawaii became the fiftieth state in the union, which increased the number of members serving in the U.S. Senate to 100. Statewide constituencies vote for senators in the same general election process used to elect representatives. Because senators

THE TWO-PARTY SYSTEM

A person elected to serve in a government office, such as a senator or a representative, is called a politician. Political parties are groups of politicians who share a fundamental governing philosophy. For the most part, the U.S. government has always been a two-party system. Although the names of the parties have changed over the years, at any one time in our history, the vast majority of government officials have represented one of two parties. Today, the two parties are the Democratic and Republican Parties. In the 109th Congress (2004–2006), only one representative and one senator represented a party other than Democratic or Republican.

The two-party system of the United States facilitates clear leadership in Congress—the political party with the most seats leads. The majority party enjoys a variety of benefits: congressional leaders, such as the Speaker of the House and Senate majority leader, represent the majority party; majority party members are awarded the majority of committee seats; and all committee chairpersons belong to the majority party. Minority party members have little or no control over the legislative agenda. The Republican Party enjoyed a slight majority in the 109th Congress, boasting 232 of 435 seats in the House of Representatives and 55 of 100 Senate seats.

serve six-year terms, though, only one-third of Senate seats are contested during an election cycle. This system of staggered term expiration allows the Senate to function consistently and avoid any major disruptions in a single election year.

The vice president of the United States also serves as president of the Senate in what is recognized as largely a ceremonial role. The vice president rarely attends Senate debates and may vote on legislation only in the event of a tie; therefore, senators elect a president *pro tempore* ("temporary president") to lead in his absence. Generally, the president pro tempore is the most senior senator in the majority party, but the role is less powerful than Speaker of the House. In fact, the president pro tempore often delegates day-to-day leadership responsibilities to junior senators to get them accustomed to Senate procedures. The leader of the Senate on any given day is referred to as the presiding officer.

Real influence in the Senate exists not at the procedural level but along political party lines. Each party elects a floor leader, commonly referred to as the majority leader (the leader of the party holding the majority of seats in the Senate), and a minority leader (leader of the party in the minority), who represent their parties as both political strategists and party spokespersons. Although these roles were not defined in the Constitution, they have evolved over time to become essential to the lawmaking process. Similar to the Speaker of the House, the majority leader has emerged as the true leader of the Senate, wielding

Above is a drawing of the Senate chamber within the Capitol building; there, the 100-member Senate meets to negotiate and debate new legislation, review proposals from the House, and carry out other official dealings.

the power to set the legislative agenda, schedule debates and votes, and influence committee assignments.

Although the Senate and the House of Representatives are equal legislative partners, the Senate is often misconstrued as the upper house of Congress. The Founding Fathers contributed to this perception by establishing the Senate as the more mature and consistent faction of Congress with a higher minimum age requirement for senators and legislative procedures that remain constant from one election year to the next. Individually, senators wield more influence than representatives simply because they serve longer terms and are fewer in number (which enables them to sit on more committees) but in fact, neither body can perform its function without the support of the other.

CONGRESSIONAL COMMITTEES

New laws originate in the form of legislation called bills. During each term, thousands of bills are introduced to Congress on a range of topics concerning every facet of American life. In order to vote on these bills in a manner that represents their constituents, senators and representatives must fully understand the potential impact of each piece of legislation. Because of the high volume of these bills, it would be impossible for individual members of Congress to investigate each one, so Congress is divided into committees that study the legislation and draft reports. All congressional members may then use these reports to become properly educated and cast informed votes.

The vast majority of new bills are addressed by standing committees. These committees are formed at the start of a congressional term and remain in service throughout the term's duration. Congressional leaders categorize incoming legislation based on subject matter, and each category is under the jurisdiction of a standing committee. Any new legislation that falls under one of these predefined categories is assigned to the corresponding standing committee for initial examination.

STANDING COMMITTEES IN THE 109TH CONGRESS

House of Representatives	Senate
Agriculture	Agriculture, Nutrition, and Forestry
Appropriations	Appropriations
Armed Services	Armed Services
Budget	Banking, Housing, and Urban Affairs
Education and the Workforce	Budget
Energy and Commerce	Commerce, Science, and Transportation
Financial Services	Energy and Natural Resources
Government Reform	Environment and Public Works
Homeland Security	Finance
House Administration	Foreign Relations

If new legislation is introduced and it does not fall under the jurisdiction of a standing committee, Congress may establish a special (or select) committee to address the bill. A special committee functions like a standing committee but disbands when its obligation is complete.

At the beginning of each new term, the Senate and the House vote on committee membership. Committee nominees are chosen by their floor leaders based on seniority and area of expertise. For example, the Judiciary Committee,

House of Representatives	Senate
International Relations	Health, Education, Labor, and Pensions
Judiciary	Homeland Security and Governmental Affairs
Resources	Judiciary
Rules	Rules and Administration
Science	Small Business and Entrepreneurship
Small Business	Veterans Affairs
Standards of Official Conduct	
Transportation and Infrastructure	
Veterans Affairs	
Ways and Means	

which oversees the administration of justice, is composed primarily of lawyers. The majority party holds a majority of seats within a committee (except in the Committee on Standards of Official Conduct, which maintains an equal number of members from each party), and the most senior member of the majority party is typically named committee chairperson. The senior member of the minority party—called the ranking member—is second in command, but the chairperson controls the legislative agenda.

EXAMPLES OF COMMITTEES AND SUBCOMMITTEES IN THE 109TH CONGRESS

House of Representatives	Senate
Commercial and Administrative Law	Banking, Housing, and Urban Affairs
The Constitution	Economic Policy
Courts, the Internet, and Intellectual Property	Financial Institutions
Crime, Terrorism, and Homeland Security	Housing and Transportation
Immigration, Border Security, and Claims	International Trade and Finance
Judiciary	Securities and Investment

Standing and select committees are further divided into subcommittees for more focused investigation of legislation under a committee's jurisdiction. When a subcommittee completes its study, it reports its findings to the committee, which may then choose to present the bill to Congress for a vote.

The organization of Congress, as defined by the U.S. Constitution in 1787, continues to provide a framework for making laws in the twenty-first century. Congress has grown and expanded along with our country's population and number of states, but its fundamental structure remains constant. When questions arise regarding the legislative process, Congress still turns to the Constitution for guidance and clarity.

The remainder of this book explains how laws are passed. The House of Representatives and the Senate are our country's lawmakers. Understanding their roles and organization is fundamental to comprehending the legislative process.

3

INTRODUCING NEW LEGISLATION

Congress undertakes a wide variety of responsibilities in its service to the U.S. government and the citizens its members represent. As defined in Article I, Section 8, of the Constitution, congressional duties include establishing new post offices and courts (with the exception of the Supreme Court), supporting the armed forces, and declaring war. The Senate must approve all presidential cabinet nominees, but only the House may impeach the president. On top of these responsibilities, the primary function of Congress is to introduce legislation and prepare bills to become law. This chapter describes the first step in creating new laws.

A new law typically originates as a piece of legislation called a bill; however, it may instead take the form of a joint resolution. Joint resolutions do not only propose new laws; they also are used to advocate constitutional amendments and declare war. The legislative procedure to propose laws is identical for joint resolutions and bills, but joint resolutions include a preamble, or introduction, which communicates the importance of passing the new law. Because joint resolutions are far less common than bills (the 108th Congress introduced 8,466 bills and only 157 joint resolutions), we refer only to bills throughout this book.

ORIGIN OF LEGISLATION

Bills may be private or public. Private bills typically provide support to individuals and groups. Federal medical benefits and immigration rights are examples of provisions that originated as private bills. The majority of bills, however, are public bills, which address the general population. Just about anyone can draft legislation describing the need for a new law, and indeed, proposals for laws originate everywhere from the president down to ordinary citizens. It is important to remember that politicians are in Congress to represent their constituents. If you have a good idea for a new law, you, too, can get involved in the legislative process.

Although anyone can propose a bill, most bills originate from members of Congress. Congressional candidates commonly have ideas for laws to improve the lives of their fellow citizens even before they are elected to office.

President Gerald Ford meets with an aide in the Oval Office, above. This office is the president's headquarters, so it is often said that things done by the president are done by the Oval Office.

These ideas make up a candidate's platform, which he or she communicates to voters while campaigning. If the voting majority agrees with a candidate's platform, that candidate will likely be elected, putting him or her in position to introduce the constituents' ideas to Congress. As a result, when the next congressional term commences, senators and representatives are already prepared to begin drafting bills on behalf of their constituents.

Other significant contributors of new legislation are lobbyists. Lobbying is the act of influencing lawmakers to support or reject legislation on behalf of interested parties. Special interest groups, such as environmentalists and labor unions, often employ professional lobbyists who are experts in drafting legislation. Lobbyists may even provide research and resources to usher bills through Congress. Many former politicians become lobbyists as a way to utilize their legislative experience in the private sector. In an effort to limit the power of lobbyists, the government imposes strict guidelines preventing these groups from providing gifts to lawmakers in exchange for legislative support.

The president of the United States, too, has ideas for new laws, and some legislation originates from the Oval Office. Once a year, when the two houses of Congress come together at the start of a new session, the president addresses the entire legislature and delivers the State of the Union address. In this speech, the president presents ideas for new legislation and follows up by submitting drafts of proposed bills to congressional leaders. During the remainder of the year, the president and other members of the executive branch may submit additional legislation to Congress to further their political agenda.

All proposed legislation eventually winds up on the desk of a senator or representative. When members of Congress receive bills originated from a third party, they may conduct additional research and amend the bills to ensure that the bills align with their platforms and the desires of their constituents. The final draft of every bill must be arranged in exactly the same way.

INTRODUCTION TO CONGRESS

Regardless of a bill's origin, whether from citizen, lobbyist, or president, only a senator or representative may introduce the new legislation to Congress. The member

THE FORMAT OF A BILL

A bill drafted in the following format is ready for introduction to Congress.

"A BILL"

[One-sentence description here]

"Be it enacted by the Senate and House of Representatives of the United States of America in Congress assembled,"

[Full text of legislation here]

of Congress who introduces the bill can be as important as the legislation itself in determining its chances to become a law. Of the 8,466 bills and 157 joint resolutions introduced to the 108th Congress, only 498 were signed into law. A bill with local impact is best introduced by the representative of the affected district, but a member of the

RESIDENT COMMISSIONER AND DELEGATES

In addition to the 435 members of the House of Representatives who represent U.S. states and congressional districts, the House includes five members who are not formal representatives. Residents of the District of Columbia, American Samoa, Guam, the U.S. Virgin Islands, and the Commonwealth of Puerto Rico are American citizens; therefore, they are eligible for representation in Congress. To that end, the Commonwealth of Puerto Rico elects a resident commissioner to the House of Representatives for a four-year term, and the four other territories elect delegates who each serve a two-year term. None of the five territories has representation in the Senate.

The resident commissioner and delegates are granted many, but not all, rights of the official representatives. They may introduce bills to the House, serve on congressional committees, and vote on committee matters. However, the resident commissioner and delegates may not vote on matters presented on the floor of the House. As a result, although these representatives can play a part in drafting and reporting legislation, they do not have a voice in determining the final approval of a bill.

relevant committee (ideally, the chairperson of that committee) should sponsor a bill that has national influence.

The senator or representative who signs the bill and introduces it to Congress is known as the primary sponsor. In order to drive a bill to approval amidst the many thousands of other bills, the primary sponsor must increase awareness of the legislation. One way to do this is by enlisting the support of cosponsors. The majority rules in Congress, so the more members who support a bill, the better chance it has of approval. The primary sponsor often shares the bill with influential members of Congress in order to recruit original cosponsors, whose names will also be listed on the bill.

Once the new bill is properly formatted and sponsored, the process for introducing it to the House of Representatives is relatively simple. The House chamber features a wooden box called "the hopper." To introduce a bill, the representative merely drops it into the hopper. The House clerk collects bills from the hopper and assigns each bill a legislative number. House legislative numbers begin with "H.R.," to indicate the bill originated in the House of Representatives, followed by a sequential numeral. For example: 5,431 of the 8,466 bills introduced during the 108th Congress originated in the House. The first of these bills was numbered H.R.1; the last was H.R.5431.

The procedure is slightly different when introducing legislation to the Senate. Typically, the sponsoring senator hands the signed document to a Senate clerk. Because fewer bills originate in the Senate, however, senators may

Above, a Senate Judiciary Committee listens to testimony on consolidation in the energy industry in March 2006. Because the issues that Congress must face are wide-ranging and complex, both the Senate and the House of Representatives divide their members into specialized committees, each of which focus on certain sets of issues.

introduce the legislation formally by reading an accompanying statement declaring the merits of the bill. On presentation of a bill, fellow senators may object to its introduction. If this happens, introduction is postponed until the next day. A second objection would bump the bill to the Senate calendar to be addressed when the majority leader sees fit. Legislative numbers for bills introduced in the Senate begin with "S."

With such a large number of bills introduced to Congress each year, similar legislation is inevitably submitted, either to a single chamber or to both the House and the Senate. Similar bills introduced concurrently to both bodies of Congress are called "companion" bills. They may be introduced coincidentally or as a tactic to increase the legislation's chances for approval. Similar bills introduced to one chamber of Congress are assigned to the same committee, where the redundancy is addressed. The committee may abandon one in favor of the other or draft an original bill based on the strongest components of each.

COMMITTEE ASSIGNMENT

Combined across the House of Representatives and the Senate, Congress operates more than 30 committees and 200 subcommittees to manage its complex workload. Standing committees are established and their members selected at the beginning of each new congressional term, which makes the process of assigning a bill to committee highly predictable and relatively simple. Most bills introduced to Congress do not propose original ideas for new laws. Instead, they modify or amend existing legislation. Therefore, new bills are assigned to the committees that dealt with related laws in the past. Once assignments are set, these bills are published and distributed to all members of Congress.

The *Congressional Record* is a continuous chronicle of all legislative action, including a verbatim account of Senate and House proceedings and committee meeting notes. Newly introduced bills, listed by their legislative numbers,

Congressman Theodore G. Bilbo reads the *Congressional Record* in March 1946. The Record is a chronicle of all legislative action, including accounts of Senate and House proceedings. The Record is distributed to members of Congress on a daily basis; it also can be accessed on the Internet.

appear in a section called the "Daily Digest." Since 1873, the Government Printing Office has distributed the *Congressional Record* on a daily basis to members of Congress for use as a resource tool. All information contained in the document is public record. Today, the *Congressional Record* is publicly available on the Internet. Interested citizens can view the document on government Web sites and stay informed of congressional activities.

The chamber's presiding officer (either the Speaker of the House or the Senate president pro tempore) refers newly logged bills to their committee assignments. A complex bill may be assigned to multiple committees, each reporting on the portion of the bill under their jurisdiction. One committee must be designated the primary committee, however, and be responsible for the bill in its entirety. For example: An animal population control bill assigned primarily to the House Agriculture Committee, which covers animals and livestock, was also referred to the Ways and Means Committee because the bill established a special state-controlled fund.

A bill referred to committee becomes the responsibility of the committee chairperson, who adds the bill to the legislative calendar and prioritizes the list of bills on the calendar. The legislative calendar is the committee's to-do list. The legislative workload remains heavy at the committee and subcommittee levels, particularly because members of Congress typically sit on multiple committees. As a result, some bills are never addressed at all. Because the chairperson always represents the majority party, this is the phase of the legislative process when the chamber majority really begins to assert its power.

If a bill's sponsor does not believe the committee chairperson is giving the legislation the attention it deserves, he or she may seek additional cosponsors to increase support for the bill. Other interested parties may get involved as well. Lobbyists, for example, often fund advertising campaigns to promote the benefits of a proposed law, and if the president supports the bill, he or she may communicate through the press the importance of quick approval. Engaged citizens may also follow a bill's progress. If they feel their elected officials are representing their political parties rather than their constituents, they too can get involved by organizing petition drives.

The three stages covered in this chapter—drafting legislation, introducing a new bill to congress, and referral to committee—are the main preparation steps in the legislative process. Once the committee chairperson adds a bill to the legislative calendar, the actual process of passing a law begins. This process was first documented in Thomas Jefferson's *A Manual of Parliamentary Practice*, which Jefferson compiled during his term as the second vice president of the United States (1797–1801) and published in 1812. In the following chapters, we will focus on a single bill and its path from committee through chamber approval to final signature.

4

CONSIDERATION
BY COMMITTEE

Every bill introduced to Congress is assigned to a committee or subcommittee and added to its legislative calendar. The primary purpose of a congressional committee is to determine whether or not a bill would make a good law. Based on that determination, the committee presents a recommendation to the chamber of Congress into which the bill was originally introduced. Only those bills valued by the committee chairperson are considered, however. A bill that is not considered will not be addressed at all by the committee. The bill simply "dies" in committee and makes no further progress toward becoming a law.

For those bills that are considered by committee, this early phase in the lawmaking process is also the most critical. As a bill progresses through Congress, it is typically amended at every stage to provide clarity, address new concerns, or document a compromise, but never is a bill under more scrutiny than during committee consideration. The assigned committee or subcommittee conducts an intensive study of each bill to understand its potential impact and determine the proposed law's necessity and feasibility of enforcement. Committees often hold public hearings to collect the facts required to make their recommendations and file committee reports.

COMMITTEE HEARINGS

Committees are usually made up of those members of Congress who have the most prior experience in the committee's field of interest. In some cases, the members of a committee themselves have the knowledge necessary to make an informed determination on a bill. If necessary, the committee may negotiate with federal agencies, such as the General Accounting Office and the President's Office of Management and Budget, to ensure that a law, if passed, will be adequately funded and supported. Complex bills, however, require additional input from experts, government officials, and other associated individuals. In order to obtain this information, the committee calls a hearing.

Committee hearings are public proceedings, similar to court trials, during which witnesses provide testimony representing all sides of a legislative issue. Unless the topic under consideration is likely to reveal classified

Above, a Senate Investigating Committee meets at the Waldorf-Astoria hotel to question individuals involved in the disastrous sinking of the ship *Titanic*. Generally, congressional committees' primary role is to review legislation; however, when circumstances demand it, ad hoc committees can be convened for investigations.

information or compromise national security, committee hearings are open to public observation. Hearing transcripts are kept for future use by committee members and distributed to other interested members of Congress. The press often reports on hearings of national interest. In fact, members of the public interested in this aspect of the legislative process may watch televised hearings on the cable network C-SPAN, which regularly broadcasts House and Senate committee proceedings.

The committee selects the witnesses it would like to testify during the hearing. Generally, there are individuals who favor a bill and those who oppose it, and a committee hears from both sides. In addition, objective experts in the field may testify on a proposed law's impact regardless of their personal opinion. If a witness chooses not to participate, the committee has the authority to serve a subpoena, forcing the potential witness to testify or face jail time. Once again, the majority party has great influence because the committee often invites more witnesses that support the majority position on the bill.

Hearings are often used as a forum for committee members to publicly present their views on an issue. Prior to witness testimony, the chairperson reads a statement expressing his or her initial thoughts. The ranking member follows with a speech from the minority point of view. Witnesses must submit their testimony to the committee in writing before the hearing. During the proceedings, the witness reads a summary and then answers questions posed by committee members. Committee rules impose a time limit on witness testimony, with each committee member receiving equal interrogation time. Once all witnesses testify, the hearing ends.

Committee hearings are an important step in the lawmaking process because they involve the participation of regular citizens in drafting legislation. By listening to the testimonials of people who would be directly affected by a new law, committee members can take into consideration the public's concerns and modify the bill to create legislation that appeals to the majority of the American people. A bill that is recommended favorably by committee is often vastly different from the draft first introduced to Congress. This is because of the inclusion of amendments to address concerns raised during hearings and those added during the markup phase.

LEGISLATION MARKUP

Following the hearings, committee members assemble for a series of markup meetings. These meetings are meant to ensure that the committee completely understands the meaning of a bill and agrees with its purpose. Armed with the testimony presented during the hearings, committee members may modify, add, and delete components of the original bill to create a version that addresses their concerns and their constituents' needs. Like committee hearings, markup meetings are held in open sessions. The proceedings are not recorded or distributed, however, which encourages lawmakers to be more candid with their concerns and more creative in exploring compromises.

Markup meetings rarely begin with a review of the legislation as originally introduced to Congress. Instead, the committee chairperson usually takes the first swipe at modifying the bill and presents to the committee what is known as the chairperson's mark. This version is the chairperson's recommendation for approval.

The amendments typically address the chairperson's own concerns as well as input from influential sources. These include majority party leadership and lobbyists with whom the chairperson may have discussed the

BYPASSING A COMMITTEE

A bill left to die in committee has one slight chance of proceeding to the full chamber for a vote. If the committee chairperson does not take action on an assigned bill for 30 or more legislative days, a member of Congress may present a motion to discharge the bill from committee. In this rarely used process, the motion remains open with the journal clerk, and members of Congress outside the committee may add their signatures in support. If a majority of the chamber into which the motion was introduced signs the document, it is entered into the *Congressional Record* and added to the Calendar of Motions to Discharge Committees.

After the measure to discharge the committee has been on the calendar for at least seven days, any signing member may call for recognition of the motion on the chamber floor. Members of the chamber debate the motion for a maximum of 20 minutes; equal time is spent arguing for and against the measure. Following the debate, a signing member may request that the chamber immediately consider the bill. If the chamber agrees to this motion, the full chamber considers the original bill under the standard legislative process, effectively bypassing committee consideration.

Senators Orrin Hatch (the ranking Republican on the Senate Committee on Finance) and Arlen Specter (chairman of the Senate Committee on Veterans Affairs) address the media during a press conference on Capitol Hill.

legislation. Although the chairperson has a powerful role, other committee members debate the changes and offer further amendments during the markup meetings.

Committee members go over the bill very carefully, reading the document line by line and discussing each line in detail before moving on to the next. If a committee member has a concern with a line, he or she may propose an amendment, such as changing a line to eliminate a conflict, adding text to clarify a definition, or removing a line altogether. The committee votes on each proposed amendment and, if approved by a majority, adds the change to the document. Any proposed amendment must be germane to the subject, which means it is directly related to the line in question.

If the committee favorably reports a heavily marked bill, the multiple amendments may actually reduce the bill's chances for approval. During the full chamber vote, members of Congress consider each amendment individually and may reject the entire legislation because of a disagreement with a single amendment. As a solution, the committee chairperson may draft a new bill that combines the text of the original with committee changes. The chairperson introduces this "clean" bill to Congress following the standard procedure. When the clean bill, under a new legislative number, is reassigned to the committee, the committee immediately reports favorably with no changes.

The legislation markup phase is the stage in the lawmaking process where most legislation is written. Bills often receive additional amendments in subsequent stages of the process, but those changes, too, must be germane to the legislation and cannot alter the overarching meaning or directive of a bill reported by committee. The influence a senator or representative wields during this process is what makes a congressional committee or subcommittee seat such a highly desirable post. During chamber sessions, members may vote on measures and offer amendment proposals, but their greatest involvement in making new laws comes during committee markup sessions.

COMMITTEE REPORT

With the markup phase complete, the committee votes to determine whether to recommend the bill to the chamber of Congress into which it was introduced. A simple majority decides the fate of the bill, and committee votes are recorded to inform the public which way each member voted. Whether the committee reports on the bill as introduced to Congress, on a marked-up version, or on a clean bill, the time spent in the hearing and markup phases is invaluable. A written report accompanying the committee's recommendation provides expert guidance

CONGRESSIONAL RECOMMENDATIONS

Committees may make one of a variety of recommendations on the bill to Congress.

Report favorably without amendment: Recommends passage of the original bill or a clean bill.

Report favorably with amendment: Recommends passage of the original bill with changes.

Report unfavorably: Recommends rejection of the bill.

Table the bill: When a committee tables a bill, it takes no further action, and the bill "dies" in committee. Committees rarely report bills unfavorably; instead, they table them—essentially rejecting the bill before it comes to a vote in the chamber.

on the proposed law and its anticipated impact on U.S. citizens.

Together with its recommendation, the committee distributes to Congress a detailed report of the bill. This report contains all the information accumulated by the committee (including transcripts of hearing proceedings and meeting notes) during its consideration and is a valuable resource for members of Congress as they prepare to vote on the bill in their respective chambers. A typical report begins with a description of the bill, the purpose of the proposed legislation, and the reasons behind the committee's recommendation. If the committee recommends a bill with amendments, each amendment is explained and the reason for its inclusion is justified.

The report also provides comprehensive information on the projected impact of the bill if passed into law. Any existing laws affected, particularly those that would be annulled, or made inoperable, by the proposed legislation, must be listed. In addition, the estimated annual costs of enforcement, projected five years into the future, must be included. Finally, the voting record of the bill is attached; this indicates how committee members voted on each amendment as well as on the final draft. In closing, committee members may add additional statements to the report. Those members who voted in the minority often take this opportunity to express their reasons for dissent.

A bill reported by committee is added to the legislative calendar of the appropriate chamber of Congress. To have adequate time to study the document before taking a final vote, members of Congress must have access to the report at least three weekdays during which Congress is in session. The committee chairperson coordinates the prompt delivery of the completed report to the Government Printing Office for distribution to all members of Congress. Today, committee reports are also made available in digital version for faster turnaround and e-mail delivery to senators and representatives who are traveling on business.

It is impossible to overstate the importance of committee consideration in passing a law, but its value truly extends beyond the legislative process. If a proposed bill becomes law, the information collected by the committee or subcommittee is included as part of its legislative history and is often revisited to serve additional purposes. For example, a committee report may be used in the judicial process as an excellent resource for interpreting the intention of the law. The work senators and representatives accomplish as members of committees is only one aspect of their roles. Equally important is time spent participating in legislative action on the House and Senate floors.

5

INITIAL HOUSE ACTION

A bill introduced to Congress is assigned to a committee, which considers the bill and then reports on it back to Congress, either favorably or adversely. If the bill is introduced in the House of Representatives, this entire process takes place in the House; if it originates in the Senate, the same process occurs in the Senate. The next three chapters of this book follow the bill as it gains approval from each chamber of Congress. Although the process is very similar in both chambers, here we will describe a bill introduced to the House, the most common path for a new law.

The House of Representatives considers a bill reported by a committee in very much the same way the committee or subcommittee addresses a bill. The main difference is the amount of time spent with the legislation. Representatives do not have adequate time to thoroughly study and debate every bill, which is why the committee report is so valuable and why noncommittee members must have the report in hand so they can read it at least three days prior to House consideration. During initial House action, the bill will be added to a legislative calendar, prioritized for consideration, presented, debated, and voted on by the chamber.

ORDER OF BUSINESS

Committees specialize in specific areas of legislation; therefore, consideration of a new bill does not vary widely from one bill to the next, and the process is fairly simple. On the House floor, however, the process is more complex because the chamber must be prepared for any type of bill—public or private, taxing or appropriation, and all others. As a result, the House employs multiple legislative calendars and other rules to prioritize and nominate bills for consideration. This strict order of business may sound confusing, but it is essential to maintaining an effective legislative process in the House.

When a bill is reported to the House of Representatives, the Speaker of the House assigns it to one of three legislative calendars: the Calendar of the Committee of the Whole House on the State of the Union (or simply the Union Calendar), the House Calendar, or the Private Calendar. The Union Calendar is used to schedule public

Newly elected Speaker of the House Nancy Pelosi, a Demo-
crat from California, is sworn in at the U.S. Capitol on
January 4, 2007. Pelosi was the first woman to be named
Speaker of the House. Pelosi and other members of Congress brought their children and grandchildren to witness the
historic event.

bills for raising revenue, apportioning funds, or authorizing payments. The House Calendar receives any public bills not covered by the Union Calendar, and the Private Calendar posts all private bills. The majority of new legislation is typically assigned to the Union Calendar.

The process to get a bill off a calendar and onto the House floor for debating is referred to as the call of committees. Every Wednesday, the Speaker of the House calls on each standing committee in order. When a committee is called, that committee's chairperson may request that the House consider any bill reported favorably by the committee that has been posted to a House calendar for at least one day. If the Speaker cannot get through all committees in a single session, the committee call resumes the following day. A committee may not be called on again until all other committees are called in the current round.

The House consideration process maintains the flow of legislation through the chamber. Although committee chairpersons have the authority to prioritize the order in which their bills are considered, their authority does not extend to the House's overall agenda. In order for a high-priority bill to reach the House floor out of order, the chairperson of the committee reporting the bill must request a resolution from the Committee on Rules calling for immediate or subsequent consideration of the bill in question. In extreme cases—known as "closed" rules—the resolution may allow a bill to bypass the House floor amendment phase.

Even with multiple legislative calendars and rules in place, the order of business may be altered by unanimous consent. On rare occasions, the Speaker of the House and the minority leader agree on a bill's importance and assign it privileged status. Bills that address national security or public health issues often fall into this category. The committee chairperson responsible for reporting a bill with privileged status may call that legislation for immediate consideration anytime during session when no other business is pending. Privileged or not, once called from the calendar, consideration of a bill begins immediately on the House floor.

HOUSE FLOOR

Any member of the House may participate in consideration of a bill on the House floor. The Speaker of the House moderates the process, and all participating representatives address only the Speaker. One majority and one minority member of the committee that reported the bill represent their respective sides as floor managers during debate. These speakers typically give a speech about the bill and then share the remainder of their allocated debate time with other interested representatives, often the author and sponsors of the bill. The consideration process differs between bills assigned to the House Calendar and those assigned to the Union Calendar.

Bills assigned to the House Calendar are not eligible for amendment. The consideration process is simple, and debate time is relatively short: After the House clerk reads the bill, speakers are granted 40 minutes, equally divided between each side of the issue, to debate the proposed legislation. Speakers use this time to present information supporting their positions on the bill in attempt to influence other representatives to vote their way. Because of the limited time for debate, some members may not have an opportunity to speak but may present a written document to ensure their positions appear in the *Congressional Record*.

Bills on the Union Calendar follow a more complex procedure, which allows for in-depth debate and amendments. To accommodate this process, the House of Representatives functions like a standing committee, called the Committee of the Whole House on the State of the Union (the Committee of the Whole). As part of this transformation, the Speaker of the House appoints a committee chairperson to run the debate, then steps down. When the Committee of the Whole completes consideration of a bill, the chamber either considers another bill from the Union Calendar or transitions back to the House of Representatives.

Consideration by the Committee of the Whole begins with the first reading of the bill. The procedure follows that of regular House debates, but each side is allowed one full hour to address the committee. Following debate, the clerk reads the bill a second time, launching the amendment phase. Like a standing committee, the Committee of the Whole reviews the bill section by section, and members may propose amendments. Only amendments that

Members of the U.S. House of Representatives walk the floor of the House chamber as they are called to vote on a resolution. After a clerk gives the final reading of the bill under consideration, the Speaker of the House immediately calls for a vote.

receive majority approval are accepted. Anytime during this phase, a member may motion to end the process. If the committee passes the motion, the bill, with all approved amendments, is read a final time.

Because of time restrictions and the high number of members seeking to participate in House action, the pace of the floor debate and consideration by the Committee of the Whole is incredibly fast. The Speaker's role as moderator is essential to maintaining order, which enables the House of Representatives to pack as much business as possible into a legislative day. The Speaker is responsible for managing the clock, approving each member who addresses the chamber, and more. Following the clerk's final reading of a bill under consideration, the Speaker immediately calls a House vote.

QUORUM

A quorum is the minimum number of participants required to conduct business. Its purpose is to encourage attendance because it enables activity to continue in a member's absence. In the U.S. Congress, a quorum is a simple majority (218 representatives or 51 senators). If the number of members present for a vote appears to be less than a quorum, the Speaker orders a quorum call, which takes the form of a roll call, conducted by the House clerk, or a recorded call using the electronic voting devices. Following the call, a present member may move to force absent members to appear in the chamber.

When the House is acting as the Committee of the Whole, only 100 representatives are needed to form a quorum. This happens because debate goes into further detail on fewer bills, so fewer members participate on each bill. If a quorum is not present, the chairperson orders a quorum call during the amendment phase, because the committee must vote on proposed amendments. In order to speed the process, the call ends as soon as it reaches 100 members. If a quorum is not reached, however, the committee rises and resolves to the House of Representatives, enabling the legislative day to continue.

VOTING PROCESS

A bill matures as it travels through the House of Representatives from introduction to vote—its content evolves with the addition of amendments that broaden the legislation's appeal. Along the way, the number of representatives backing the bill grows. Introduced by a single member of Congress, the bill likely picked up cosponsors before becoming the focus of a committee. It leaves the committee with the backing of a political party, and is finally considered by an entire chamber that is well versed with the bill's contents through the committee report. A vote determines if the bill has support from the majority of the House.

The call for a House vote is a routine action. The Speaker asks, "As many as are in favor of [name of the bill], say 'Aye.' As many as are opposed, say 'No.'" All members of the House of Representatives present in the chamber may vote on the bill. Bills assigned to the House Calendar require a three-fifths majority in order to pass. For example, if 100 people vote, 60 of them must be in favor to approve a bill. A bill called from the Union Calendar, however, needs only a simple majority (e.g., 51 out of 100) to be approved.

The Speaker determines the result by the response volume. If he or she hears more "Ayes" than "Nos," the Speaker declares the bill passed. When a vote is too close to call, the Speaker may order a division vote, in which representatives stand up rather than call out to cast their votes. The Speaker counts standing members to calculate the vote. The final option is an electronic

Above is an 1890 photograph of the House of Representatives chamber, taken from the balcony while the House was in session. Today, many House votes are taken as they would have been in 1890, with the passage of a bill determined by the response volume of "Ayes" versus "Nos."

vote. Representatives cast their votes using an electronic voting station, which counts automatically and accurately. This method is foolproof, but because there are a limited number of voting stations, it is time consuming, so it is rarely used.

Bills that make it to a vote are important to the parties that supported them through the legislative process. If that party is the voting minority, it has an opportunity to keep the bill alive. The bill's floor manager may call a motion to reconsider the bill and try to win a future vote. The Speaker typically grants this request without debate and reassigns the bill to committee. A representative interested in adding a final amendment may motion to recommit with instructions. This motion is debatable, as both parties wish to influence what instructions appear when the bill is reconsidered.

Representatives are the voices of the people in Congress, and they are elected for two basic reasons: to draft legislation that benefits the constituents of their congressional districts and all United States citizens, and to represent constituents' interests when voting on other new laws under consideration. Politics are built on the foundation of compromise, however, and in order for representatives to get things done, at times they must give other members of Congress what they need—votes. Fortunately, legislators have a couple of tricks they can use to help a fellow member without voting against the interests of their own constituents.

In a "catch-and-release" deal, to "catch" the number required for a majority, a party leader persuades minority representatives to promise their votes. Although their constituents might disapprove, these representatives may agree, in exchange for guaranteed future votes from the majority party. If the leader secures more votes than required, however, the representative is "released" from the deal. Then, the bill passes, and the member votes as his constituents expect. Pairing is another method. A representative persuaded to vote against his constituents' desires pairs up with a member on the opposite side. Both vote "Present," rather than in favor or opposition; these votes do not change the outcome, but the representative does not record a vote unpopular with his constituents.

6

SENATE REVIEW

A bill introduced to and passed by the House of Representatives is referred to the Senate for consideration. It is important to remember that the Senate and the House are equal partners in passing legislation. The Senate does not review House bills as a superior body of Congress; it reviews them from a different perspective. Whereas House members represent proportional numbers of constituents, senators represent states equally. By the same token, the House reviews all bills introduced and passed in the Senate. Similar to initial House action, review by the Senate involves committee consideration, floor debates and amendments to the bill, and chamber votes.

In general, the Senate consideration process is very similar to the House process, as both are based on Thomas Jefferson's *Manual of Parliamentary Practice*. The House reasserts its procedural rules at the start of each new Congress. By contrast, the Senate functions largely by the rules established during the first Congress in 1789, and the manner in which business is conducted is quite different from the House. Pace of activity is another key difference. Because there are fewer members generating legislation, more committee assignments per senator, and longer debate times, the Senate pace is much slower than that of the House.

REFERRAL TO SENATE

When a bill passes a body of Congress, it formally becomes an act. Immediately upon approval, the House sends a written message to the Senate chamber indicating the change of status, and the Senate prepares to receive an engrossed copy of the act for review. The engrossed copy is a final version of the legislation prepared by the House enrolling clerk. It is crucial that the engrossed copy contains the text of the bill exactly as approved by the House because both bodies of Congress must pass completely identical versions in order to advance the legislation to the next step.

To draft an engrossed copy of a bill, the enrollment clerk combines the version reported by the standing committee with the amendments approved during initial House action. The enrollment clerk pays special attention to the order in which the amendments were introduced and the precise wording and punctuation agreed to by House members. This process can be quite challenging, particularly with a heavily amended bill. Today, some bills receive more than 100 amendments, pushing the average length of a bill to more than 19 pages. An engrossed act received by the secretary of the Senate is ready for committee assignment.

The Senate has fewer standing committees than the House, but the committee consideration process is the same in each chamber. Sometimes, however, identical bills are introduced in both places at the same time, to increase the chances of passing. These are called companion bills. If the companion bill is approved by the House and assigned to a Senate committee, the committee indefinitely postpones the Senate version and considers only the approved House act. If the Senate is considering a similar bill when the House bill passes, the Senate committee may add elements of its bill to the House act in the form of amendments.

At the close of the committee consideration phase, the assigned Senate committee prepares a report and presents the legislation to the Senate floor. As described in Chapter 3, the act may be reported favorably or adversely, clean or with amendments. During the opening proceedings of each new legislative day, the presiding officer calls for the filing of committee reports. At this time, the committee representative may speak to the chamber about the act and communicate his or her position. However, this opportunity is rarely taken, and senators typically hand the report to a chamber clerk in document form.

Legislative days are different from calendar days; a legislative day is a period of conducting business. A new legislative day begins when the previous one adjourns,

Senator Robert Byrd of Tennessee celebrates after winning his record ninth term. Byrd became the president *pro tempore* of the Senate in January 2007 and was the Senate majority leader for two separate terms during his tenure.

as indicated by the presiding officer, who declares an official order to indicate the close of business. At the end of a calendar day, if the Senate is in the midst of conducting business, the presiding officer may call a recess to allow the Senate staff to go home. A recess is simply a pause in the proceedings. In the morning, the Senate continues its work. When business is complete, the presiding officer adjourns the legislative day. Legislative days may last several calendar days or even weeks.

SENATE CHAMBER

Although the legislative procedure of the Senate is similar to that of the House, the manner in which the Senate conducts business is substantially different. In the House, strict adherence to the rules is necessary to manage a large chamber with 435 members generating thousands of bills every session. In the Senate, with 100 senators serving six-year terms, the order of business can be more flexible. Senators actually have more influence over the flow of legislation than the presiding officer, which is in stark contrast to the House of Representatives, where the Speaker tightly controls the order of business.

The Senate maintains one calendar to track legislation, the Calendar of Business, on which all introduced bills and approved acts appear, regardless of type. Each legislative day, as part of morning business, the presiding officer conducts the call of the calendar, which is a process to address pending business. When the next reported act comes up, if there are no objections, the chamber may begin consideration. This rule, however, is rarely used. Senators usually prefer to waive the calendar call in favor of addressing legislation in order of priority or efficiency.

To address an act outside the order prescribed by the Calendar of Business, a senator presents a motion to the presiding officer to consider the legislation. A motion is commonly used to consider an uncomplicated act immediately after its report, and requires unanimous consent from the Senate chamber. If granted, the presiding officer allocates time for debate, and floor consideration begins. If another senator objects to the motion, the act remains on the Calendar of Business and may be taken up during a future call. If the Senate requires no debate or amendments, a quick vote removes the act from the calendar.

Motions to consider legislation out of order are typically made by the Senate majority leader. Although the Senate does not adhere to its legislative calendar as strictly as the House of Representatives, there is an order of business,

SYSTEM OF LIGHTS AND BELLS

Senators and representatives are busier than ever before. The average hours spent working per week, days per year, and bills introduced per Congress have increased greatly over time. Because of the heavy workload and the fact that sessions may operate with only a quorum present, senators and representatives appear in their respective chambers only when required to do so. More often, they can be found working in their offices or other parts of the Capitol building, so Congress utilizes a system of lights and bells that signal throughout these areas to inform members of Congress of important developments in the chambers.

The tools of the system are simple enough (consisting of a bell and two lights, side by side). The system itself is complex, however, because of the many combinations of rings and lights necessary to communicate the various messages, particularly in the House, which includes specific codes for the Committee of the Whole. Utilizing this system, messages can be communicated to absent legislators regarding quorum calls, votes, adjournment, recess, and more. When a recorded vote is called, the alert is sent after the first member registers a vote. Remaining members have 15 minutes in which to appear in the chamber and record their votes.

which is unofficially controlled by the majority leader. The majority leader meets regularly with members of his or her party and the minority leader to identify Senate priorities and agree on which acts to consider next. This type of process works well in the Senate, where agendas, as well as the deals brokered around each new piece of legislation, change on a daily basis.

When a motion to consider an act receives unanimous consent, it is usually not a surprise—in fact, very few legislative bombshells get dropped on the Senate floor, thanks to the work of the Republican Legislative Scheduling Office and the Democratic Policy Committee. These service groups partner with their respective party members and leaders to facilitate communication regarding legislative issues, priorities, and procedural plans. They provide the information that party leaders need to devise their floor strategies, down to predicted senator responses to motions. Political party alignment becomes even more important when the Senate chamber considers an act for approval.

FLOOR CONSIDERATION

Once an act is recognized for consideration, one senator from each party represents his or her side of the issue as floor managers throughout the debate. These senators are typically the chairperson and ranking member of the committee that holds jurisdiction over the act. Floor managers speak first and then yield the floor to other senators, usually members of the same party, who present prepared statements in support of their positions on the act. Senate

Incoming Senate majority leader Harry Reid *(right)*, accompanied by incoming Senate minority leader Mitch McConnell, gestures during a news conference on January 4, 2007.

rules impose no limits on the number of senators who may speak or the length of their speeches. This is a significant and noticeable difference between the two chambers of Congress.

The primary goal of speaking during floor debate is to win the votes of any undecided senators. Presentations often include facts and charts, based on research data collected during committee hearings, to illustrate important points. Senate debate is a public event, which is broadcast live on the cable television channel C-SPAN2. The proceedings are recorded and printed in the *Congressional Record,* which is also available to read online at the Library of Congress Web site. Although senators may address only the presiding officer during debate, they use this opportunity to sway public opinion as well as that of their colleagues.

Sometimes, the goal of speaking during debate is delaying the vote. Senators on the minority side typically state their cases and graciously accept defeat, but occasionally, when they are ardently opposed to an act, they use the only tool available to halt the process—the filibuster. Because Senate rules do not limit speech length, senators may delay a vote by simply speaking at great length. In 1957, South Carolina Senator Strom Thurmond spoke nonstop for over 24 hours in opposition to a proposed law. This tactic is most effective with a united political party, but even a single senator can make an impact.

Eventually, both sides in the debate complete their arguments for and against the act, and the floor managers yield their time back to the presiding officer. The presiding officer then requests the final reading of the act and calls for a vote. The Senate usually employs the roll call voting method, in which the legislative clerk reads each senator's name in alphabetical order, and the senator responds "aye" in favor of the legislation or "no" in opposition. The Senate requires a simple majority to pass an act and, as in the House of Representatives, a quorum is required to vote.

The presiding officer votes only to break a tie. When all votes are calculated and a result determined, the presiding officer announces the act's passage or defeat. Following the announcement, the party leader for the losing side typically requests a motion to reconsider the act. This motion is a mere formality, though, as the majority side simply tables it, thus marking the vote as the final Senate action for the legislation in its present form. If the Senate passed the act, the next step in its journey toward becoming law depends on whether or not the Senate amended the legislation.

A proposed law must pass both the House of Representatives and the Senate in identical form to receive congressional approval. If the Senate passed the act without amendment, then the legislation is approved for submission to the White House and presidential action. If the Senate edited or modified the act in any way, however, the legislation returns to the House for final review and vote on the amended version. Most new laws require a return to the chamber of introduction. This book assumes a Senate-modified act, so our legislation along with Senate amendments returns to the House of Representatives.

7

FINAL
CONGRESSIONAL
APPROVAL

A bill introduced into the House of Representatives and passed by the House is then submitted to the Senate for consideration. The Senate often changes the House-approved act based on new information discovered during committee hearings, fresh perspectives argued in debate, or related ideas in pending legislation, and votes on an edited version. These changes, known as amendments, may take the form of a word or section added to the act, removed, or edited to alter its meaning. Ideally, through effective negotiation and amendments, legislators will broaden an act's appeal until majorities in both chambers support its passage into law.

Following Senate approval, the amended act is returned to the House of Representatives. The importance of reconsideration by the House cannot be overemphasized. A single amendment may significantly alter the nature of an act, and, on occasion, individual pieces of legislation have been amended up to 500 times! In one peculiar instance, amendments to the Tax Reform Act of 1986 modified the original bill such that the price of season tickets to both University of Texas and Louisiana State University football games became tax deductible. Final congressional approval provides an opportunity for every member of Congress to gain an understanding of all amendments.

RETURN TO THE HOUSE

The Senate prepares an engrossed version of the act, which includes all amendments in a comprehensive, final document, and delivers this legislation directly to the Speaker of the House. The House of Representatives has a wide variety of available actions with which to address a Senate-amended act. One rarely used action is the motion to resubmit the act to the standing committee or subcommittee that initially considered the House-approved version. Rather than return the act to committee, the committee chairperson evaluates the complexity of amendments in the engrossed act and considers the updated legislation in the Committee of the Whole.

If the chairperson agrees with the Senate amendments and approves of their impact on the nature of the legislation, he or she may recommend that the House accept the engrossed act as is. The chairperson consults the other committee or subcommittee members and, with their support, motions to request a House vote on the act. The Speaker of the House calls for a chamber vote and, if the engrossed act passes without objection, the legislation has achieved approval from both chambers of Congress. The proposed law is ready for enrollment and submission for presidential action.

Because of concerns with one or more Senate amendments, the House might not unanimously pass the engrossed act. If this happens, then the chairperson may "motion to amend the amendments." In this action, the Committee of the Whole considers each Senate amendment individually. The chairperson deletes, modifies, or approves amendments until the House reaches agreement on the legislation and passes it without objection. Because the Senate's engrossed act has changed, the House must resubmit its amended version to the Senate to secure approval of identical legislation. If this act passes the Senate without objection, then it is ready for presidential action.

Sometimes the chairperson believes the Senate amendments went too far, altering the House-approved act so that it no longer reflects the spirit of the original legislation. In these cases, the chairperson, with the support of the committee or subcommittee members, may "motion to call a Conference Committee" to consider the legislation. A

Conference Committee is a temporary committee made up of both Senate and House members. The purpose of this committee is to prepare a compromised version of the act,

HIGH-SCHOOL STUDENTS IN CONGRESS

Working as a congressional page provides the ultimate perspective for young people interested in observing our government's lawmaking process. The first page was nine-year-old Grafton Hanson, who was appointed in 1827. Today, Congress employs more than 100 pages in the two houses. Pages are responsible for preparing the chambers for each day's session and providing general assistance to legislators and chamber staff. Pages are most often seen running documents between chambers, congressional offices, and other government buildings. Their presence enables lawmakers to focus on the business at hand, transitioning from one bill to the next without a lapse in productivity.

All pages must be high-school juniors during their time of service, which may include summer sessions before or after their junior years. In addition to working in Congress, pages enjoy preferred access to Washington, D.C., area museums and other points of interest. To become a page, a student must be nominated by a senator or representative from his or her state of residence. Additional requirements include maintaining a 3.0 GPA, providing letters of recommendation, writing an essay, and participating in an interview process. If you wish to be a page, contact your state's congressional members to request a nomination.

which may be accepted in identical form by both chambers of Congress. The next section explains this process in detail.

A motion to call a Conference Committee may be made only by the chamber of Congress in possession of the legislation at the time of the motion (and this is not always the House of Representatives). During initial review in the Senate, the committee chairperson may recognize that because of extensive amendments, the Senate version is not likely to pass the House as is. In this case, the Senate majority leader, on submitting the engrossed bill to the House, may motion to call a Conference Committee, thus placing negotiation in the hands of the Conference Committee and disabling the House chairperson's option to amend Senate amendments.

CONFERENCE COMMITTEE

Often referred to as the "Third House of Congress," a Conference Committee is itself a powerful legislative body focused on advancing acts deadlocked between the Senate and the House of Representatives. After the second chamber agrees to the requesting chamber's motion for a Conference Committee, the Speaker of the House and Senate presiding officer select committee members to address the act under consideration. The conference may convene a single time or conduct a series of meetings. Once the conference comes to a compromise, it submits its recommendation in the form of a report to both chambers of Congress, and the committee is dissolved.

Although the Conference Committee meets as one entity, it is actually made up of two subgroups representing the House and the Senate. Each body assigns a number of its members (usually, 7–11) to the conference. Conference Committee members are called managers or, more informally, "conferees." The number of conferees in a subgroup is not significant because when called upon to make a decision on an amendment, the groups each vote with a single voice. Conference members must work within their group to come to a majority decision, which is then communicated as that congressional body's united position on the issue.

Because of the importance of Conference Committee decisions, the majority party leaders in each body (Speaker of the House and Senate presiding officer) handpick the conferees. Senior members of the committees that considered the act under its initial review in the House and the Senate, such as the committee chairpersons and ranking members, are typically appointed, and chairpersons may be advised by other chamber members on additional members. When an act is of particular interest to the majority party, though, the party leaders are sure to assign legislators whom they expect will promote an outcome that is most beneficial to majority party interests.

The Conference Committee receives the engrossed act and any further amendments. Seeking to eliminate disputes, the committee considers only controversial amendments. It may not alter sections agreed to by both chambers. Any compromise the committee suggests must be germane

A 16-year-old girl and a 17-year-old boy listen to the floor debate in the state senate chambers in Jackson, Mississippi. Teenagers like this also serve as pages in the U.S. Congress; their duties include preparing the chambers for each day's session and providing general assistance, like running documents between chambers and other government offices.

to the act, meaning it must not introduce new information. If an issue under dispute is a number (for example, an amendment changed a 5 to a 10), the committee must agree on a figure between 5 and 10. If an issue is in the text, the amendment must be rewritten to the approval of the conference without adding content nonexistent elsewhere in the document.

After the Conference Committee considers the engrossed act, it reports to Congress its recommendation for advancement of the legislation. The conference addresses each disputed amendment based on the following four options:

1. The Senate recede from all (or certain of) its amendments.
2. The House recede from its disagreement to all (or certain of) the Senate amendments and agree thereto.
3. The House recede from its disagreement to all (or certain of) the Senate amendments and agree thereto with amendments.
4. The House recede from all (or certain of) its amendments to the Senate amendments or its amendments to the Senate bill.

If the Conference Committee cannot agree on some amendments, the report must include a statement explaining the conflicting recommendations. If, after a period of 20 calendar days and 10 legislative days, the conference reaches no agreement at all, replacement conferees are appointed to keep the negotiations moving forward. Once complete, a majority of each conference group signs the report, which is printed and distributed to each chamber of Congress. The final report is a detailed document that describes Conference Committee recommendations and their impact on the legislation. This document is the basis for final congressional consideration of the act.

FINAL CONSIDERATION

A Conference Committee report contains joint recommendations from the two bodies of Congress for reconciling amendments to an act that were not initially agreed to by both chambers. If both bodies agree to the recommendations, then the act takes the next step toward becoming law. The chambers consider the report individually, beginning with the body that *accepted* the Conference Committee request. In the House, the report must be printed in the *Congressional Record* three calendar days prior to consideration to allow adequate preparation and debate. The Senate, which does not debate conference reports prior to consideration, may address the report immediately.

Conference report consideration is a high priority in both houses. Once available for consideration in the House or the Senate, the presiding officer typically addresses the report as the next order of business. Debate in the House is limited to one hour, equally divided between the majority and minority parties. If the House floor managers for each party agree in their support of the report, then any opposing members may represent the dissenting position for one-third of the allotted debate time. A conference report may not be amended during consideration; following debate, the chamber votes on adoption of the report as is.

If the first chamber to act on the conference report votes to reject its recommendations, then the report returns to the Conference Committee for further negotiation. If the chamber accepts the report, however, the official papers are submitted to the second body for consideration. Following approval, the first chamber's group of conferees officially disbands, having fulfilled its duty. If the second chamber votes to accept the report, then the act has passed Congress and is prepared for presidential action. Because the first chamber disbanded its conferees, if rejected by the second chamber, the act cannot be recommitted to conference, so a motion is made for a new Conference Committee to consider the act.

If a report under consideration includes conflicting recommendations, then after voting on the report, the chambers must vote on each disputed amendment. If the voting body submitted an amendment in question, that chamber may withdraw the amendment to resolve the issue. If the other body submitted the amendment, the voting body may accept or amend the amendment and hope the other body accepts the change. If the chambers still cannot agree, the entire Conference Committee process begins again. It is possible that the congressional session may end while an act is under consideration. If this happens, then the legislation dies and must be reintroduced in the next session.

In the most typical scenario, both chambers of Congress accept the Conference Committee report, thus passing the act in identical form in each house. With this milestone met, all original papers generated during the legislative process are delivered to the originating chamber of Congress and submitted to the enrolling clerk. The enrolling clerk prepares a clean version of the approved act in its final form and submits the document to the Government Printing Office, which prepares on parchment the official legislation for presidential action. At the close of the congressional session, all original papers are filed in the National Archives.

When you consider the various checks and balances available to lawmakers during the final approval stage, you begin to understand the intricacies of the legislative process. This complexity ensures that any legislation reaching the President's desk has been very carefully considered from multiple perspectives—should it become law, it will be as fair as possible to the American people. On the other hand, the entire process can be simple, particularly when the same majority party with shared priorities leads both chambers. It is important to note that Congress submits legislation for presidential action as a *recommendation*. The president, too, plays a powerful role in passing new laws.

8

PRESIDENTIAL
ACTION

Presidential action takes place at the end of the process by which a bill passes into law, but the president's influence can be felt all along the way. At the beginning of each calendar year, the president stands before both chambers of Congress as a whole to deliver the State of the Union address. The address usually includes a look back at America's progress over the previous 12 months and a look forward, outlining presidential expectations from Congress in the coming year. During this speech, the president asks Congress to introduce and pass what he envisions as the legislation of greatest importance to the nation.

Throughout the legislative process, the president may attempt to persuade members of Congress to vote in support of bills on his or her agenda. One tactic the president uses to sway a legislator's vote is federal funds allocation. For example, a representative who provides the president with a key vote may in turn be granted finances to support a vital program for his or her constituents. When the president and congressional majorities are of the same political party, they can partner to deliver a unified agenda. Historically, this has rarely been the case, making presidential action another procedural check and balance.

LEGISLATIVE OPTIONS

Traditionally, the enrolled act is signed first by the Speaker of the House and then by the president of the Senate (the vice president, if available, or the president pro tempore). After these signatures are obtained, the act returns to the chamber of its origin, where either the House clerk or secretary of the Senate submits the document to the White House. On receipt of the act by a White House clerk, the president has 10 days in which to take action. During this time, the president may have the act distributed to cabinet members who oversee related departments for their advisement.

If the president agrees with the act in its submitted form, he may pass it into law simply by signing and dating the document. A messenger communicates the news to the House and Senate chambers, and the signed document is delivered to the archivist of the United States, where the new law receives an official number. Laws are designated

President Lyndon Johnson signs into law the Civil Rights Act of 1964. The president plays an integral role in lawmaking; each law requires his or her signature before it is considered to be official.

by their private or public status, the congressional session, and the order in which they passed. For example, the first public law passed in the 109th Congress is numbered *Public Law 109-1*, the second is *Public Law 109-2*, and so on.

If the president disagrees with an enrolled act, he may refuse to sign it and instead veto the act or simply ignore it. A veto is a complete rejection of the act. Rather than signing the act into law, the president returns it to Congress with a veto message, which communicates the reasons why he or she did not sign the law. Often, the president is well aware of legislation under consideration in Congress, and if he or she disagrees with an act, Congress may be informed of plans for a presidential veto. This threat of veto can influence legislators to address the president's concerns prior to submitting the act.

An act vetoed by the president and retuned to Congress is not necessarily dead. Congress has the power to overturn a veto. If both chambers of Congress vote to accept the act by two-thirds majorities, the act becomes law without the president's signature. Then, the new law bypasses a second presidential action and is submitted to the archivist. If the act does not receive the required two-thirds majority in each chamber, however, it may be resubmitted for committee consideration to amend the sections disagreed to by the president. The act must be approved once again by both houses in identical form before resubmitting to the president.

If the president chooses to ignore an enrolled act, his or her inaction does not halt the process. By not taking direct action on a bill, the president is in effect passively taking action. From the time a White House clerk receives the act, the president has a 10-day deadline in which to either sign or veto the legislation. If the 10-day period expires before the president takes action, the act automatically becomes law without the president's signature. Typically, the president allows this to happen when he or she does not personally agree with the legislation, but the act has

LINE-ITEM VETO

For a brief period between 1997 and 1998, the president had an additional legislative option called the "line-item veto." The line-item veto, which is used by many governors when addressing state legislation, enabled then-president Bill Clinton to consider an act line by line and to cancel certain elements with which he did not agree. President Clinton would then sign the act into law and return the deleted sections to Congress, which could vote to overturn the president's decisions just as it would with a standard veto. The line-item veto, as defined, limited the president's power so that he could cancel only certain types of fiscal items.

The purpose of the line-item veto was to enable the President to eliminate region-specific (also known as "pork barrel") benefits from national laws. President Bill Clinton (1992–2000) was the only president to employ the line-item veto, which he used 11 times during its existence to cancel 82 items. On June 25, 1998, in the case of *Clinton v. City of New York*, the U.S. Supreme Court ruled the line-item veto unconstitutional, thus eliminating the option. It is interesting to note that in 1861, secessionists wrote similar presidential power into the Constitution of the Confederate States of America.

enough public support that vetoing it would reflect poorly on the president's popularity.

Unresolved bills do not carry over from one congressional session to the next, so an act received by the White House with fewer than 10 days remaining in the session is in a perilous position. Under this circumstance, if the president disagrees with the act, he can actually kill the legislation by taking no action—this is known as a "pocket veto." The president does not sign the act. It is not vetoed, so Congress cannot overturn the decision, and as the session expires, the legislation dies. In order to submit an identical act, Congress must start from scratch during its next session.

COMMUNICATION AND ENFORCEMENT

Whether enacted into law by the president's signature, congressional override of a veto, or 10-day period expiration, the new law receives its official number from the archivist of the United States, and is ready for publication. In an effort to communicate new laws as quickly and effectively as possible, the government publishes the legislation in three variations: slip laws, *United States Statutes at Large,* and United States Code. These formats are not direct channels to the general public, however, so we typically rely on the media, our local officials, or government resources such as the Library of Congress to follow legislative updates.

Prepared by the Office of the Federal Register, National Archives and Records Administration, within a few days of its enactment, the slip law is typically the first publication of a new law. The slip law is a document that contains the complete text of the law along with a comprehensive list of facts (including dates the bill passed each chamber of Congress, which committees considered the legislation, and its inclusion in the Congressional Record) chronicling

SIGNING STATEMENTS

During presidential action, when the president signs an act, he or she may attach a message known as a signing statement. Originally, the signing statement was designed to be a brief interpretation of the president's expected outcome of the law, an advisory note to the president's staff on enforcement, or a concern about the law's constitutionality. Any of these statements are valid; however, it is the judiciary's role to determine the constitutionality of our laws in practice. Things get tricky when the president believes a law to be unconstitutional and pledges in his signing statement not to enforce certain sections.

The signing statement was first used by President James Monroe (1817–1825). By 1980, only 75 total signing statements had been issued. Use and influence of these often-controversial notes have increased dramatically during recent administrations, however. Today, signing statements are added to a law's legislative history for consultation during judicial interpretation. As of 2006, President George W. Bush (2000–2008) had personally issued more than 130 signing statements, identifying 750 unconstitutional elements in acts he signed into law. Signing statements, it seems, have replaced the line-item veto as a tactic for customizing laws to a president's demands.

Supreme Court justice Felix Frankfurter holds a book of statutes in his office in this 1957 photograph. The *U.S. Statutes at Large* contain the full text of every law, public and private, ever passed by the U.S. government.

its legislative history. Copies of the slip law are available to officials and the public through the document rooms of either house of Congress or directly from the Government Printing Office.

First printed in 1845, the *United States Statutes at Large* is a series of large, hardbound volumes that contains the full text of every law, public and private, ever passed by the U.S. government. At the end of each session of Congress, a new volume is added to the series, which includes all laws passed during the session, in the order in which they were enacted. When a new law is added to the *Statutes at*

Large, its entry includes notes identifying precedent-setting legislation and cross references for simple location of relevant laws elsewhere in the *Statutes at Large.*

The United States Code contains all public laws in a condensed format, organized by title and section. This is the law resource used most frequently by officials who reference public laws on a daily basis. A new law is codified by the addition of numbers that refer to the corresponding title and section of the U.S. Code. These reference numbers then appear in the margins of the slip law and the *Statutes at Large.* The Law Revision Counsel of the House of Representatives publishes a new edition of the U.S. Code every six years, and a supplement featuring new laws passed during the term is released after each congressional session. In order to be effective, new laws must be simultaneously communicated to all levels of society. Judges who preside over the relevant area of law must become familiar enough with its text and history to interpret the law's intent and apply broad legislation to specific cases. Law enforcement agencies with jurisdiction over the particular law must be prepared to recognize an abuse of it and identify exactly which section of the U.S. Code is in violation, sometimes under highly stressful circumstances. Finally, the general public must be informed to know how to function within the boundaries of the law.

Upon enactment of a new federal law and communication through the various official channels, the law becomes the responsibility of the third branch of the U.S. government: the judiciary. The U.S. Supreme Court, the

Above is a view of the U.S. Supreme Court building, where the eight associate justices and the chief justice conduct their day-to-day business. The Supreme Court has an important role regarding the law—when a law is challenged, it is up to the Court to determine if the law at issue is constitutional.

court of appeals, and district courts have jurisdiction over federal laws. Judges who preside over these courts must be nominated by the president and confirmed by the Senate. The courts enforce laws based on constitutionality, but judges continually apply new thinking and precedent-setting legislation to interpret laws based on the standards of the day. A law may be changed or repealed only through the legislative process.

CONCLUSION

Existing laws are constantly challenged by the changing times, from shifting public priorities to emerging technologies. Music copyright laws are a perfect example. Congress passed its first music copyright laws in the 1800s—prior to the existence of the recording industry—to protect songwriters' rights to sheet music. The recording industry emerged

PUBLIC LAW CODES

Every public law is coded under one of the following categories:

Title 1	General Provisions	**Title 13**	Census
Title 2	The Congress	**Title 14**	Coast Guard
Title 3	The President	**Title 15**	Commerce and Trade
Title 4	Flag and Seal, Seat of Government, and the States	**Title 16**	Conservation
Title 5	Government Organization and Employees	**Title 17**	Copyrights
Title 6	Domestic Security	**Title 18**	Crimes and Criminal Procedure
Title 7	Agriculture	**Title 19**	Custom Duties
Title 8	Aliens and Nationality	**Title 20**	Education
Title 9	Arbitration	**Title 21**	Food and Drugs
Title 10	Armed Forces	**Title 22**	Foreign Relations and Intercourse
Title 11	Bankruptcy	**Title 23**	Highways
Title 12	Banks and Banking	**Title 24**	Hospitals and Asylums
		Title 25	Indians

in the twentieth century, and copyright laws evolved to take into consideration recorded music for purchase and broadcast. Today, in the twenty-first century, Congress struggles

Title 26 Internal Revenue Code

Title 27 Intoxicating Liquors

Title 28 Judiciary and Judicial Procedure

Title 29 Labor

Title 30 Mineral Lands and Mining

Title 31 Money and Finance

Title 32 National Guard

Title 33 Navigation and Navigable Waters

Title 34 Navy (repealed)

Title 35 Patents

Title 36 Patriotic Societies and Observances

Title 37 Pay and Allowances of the Uniformed Services

Title 38 Veterans' Benefits

Title 39 Postal Service

Title 40 Public Buildings, Property, and Works

Title 41 Public Contracts

Title 42 The Public Health and Welfare

Title 43 Public Lands

Title 44 Public Printing and Documents

Title 45 Railroads

Title 46 Shipping

Title 47 Telegraphs, Telephones, and Radiotelegraphs

Title 48 Territories and Insular Possessions

Title 49 Transportation

Title 50 War and National Defense

to adapt music copyright laws to a landscape encompassing everything from digital downloads to satellite radio to ring tones for your mobile phone.

The U.S. government's procedure for creating, amending, and passing new laws, however, remains constant. When the process is respected and adhered to by all parties, it is a near flawless system: checks and balances across three branches of government; equal representation of the people, with opportunities for participation by engaged citizens; meticulous consideration and spirited debate over new legislation; and a Constitution against which to appraise new laws as they apply to specific situations. The process has been sturdy enough to serve as our country's cornerstone for more than two centuries and is flexible enough to carry us confidently into the future.

GLOSSARY

amendment A proposal to alter the text of a pending bill or other measure by striking out some of it, by inserting new language, or both. Before an amendment becomes part of the measure, the Senate or House must agree to it.

clean bill After a committee has amended legislation, the chairman may be authorized by the panel to assemble the changes and what remains unchanged from the original bill and then reintroduce everything as a clean bill. A clean bill may expedite Senate or House action by avoiding separate floor consideration of each amendment.

Congressional Record The substantially verbatim account of daily proceedings on the Senate or House floor. It is printed for each calendar day Congress is in session. At the back of each daily issue is the "Daily Digest," which summarizes the day's floor and committee activities.

consideration To "call up" or "lay down" a bill or other measure on the Senate or House floor is to place it before the full chamber for consideration, including debate, amendment, and voting.

engrossed bill   The official copy of a bill or joint resolution passed by the Senate or House and certified by the Secretary of the Senate or House Clerk.

enrolled bill   The final copy of a bill or joint resolution that has passed both chambers in identical form. It is printed on parchment paper, signed by appropriate House and Senate officials, and submitted to the President for signing.

floor   Action "on the floor" is that which occurs as part of a formal session of a full chamber. An action "from the floor" is one taken by a senator or representative during a session of Congress. A senator or representative who has been recognized to speak by the chair is said to "have the floor."

legislative day   A "day" that begins when the chamber meets after an adjournment and ends when the chamber next adjourns. Hence, a legislative day may extend over several calendar days or even weeks and months.

override of a veto   The process by which each chamber of Congress votes on a bill vetoed by the President. To pass a bill over the President's objections requires a two-thirds vote in each chamber. Historically, Congress has overridden fewer than 10 percent of all presidential vetoes.

pocket veto   The Constitution grants the President 10 days to review a measure passed by the Congress. If the President has not signed the bill after 10 days, it becomes law without his signature. If Congress adjourns during the 10-day period, however, the bill does not become law, a result known as a pocket veto.

president pro tempore A constitutionally recognized officer of the Senate who presides over the chamber in the absence of the vice president. The president pro tempore (or, "president for a time") is elected by the Senate and is, by custom, the senator of the majority party with the longest record of continuous service.

private law A private bill enacted into law. Private laws have restricted applicability, often addressing immigration and naturalization issues affecting individuals.

public law A public bill or joint resolution that has passed both chambers and been enacted into law. Public laws have general applicability nationwide.

quorum The number of members that must be present for the Senate or House to do business. The Constitution requires a majority of senators (51) or representatives (218) for a quorum. Often, fewer members are actually present on the floor, but the chamber presumes that a quorum is present unless the contrary is shown by a roll call vote or quorum call.

select or special committee A committee established for a limited time period to perform a particular study or investigation. These committees might be given or denied authority to report legislation to the Senate or House.

slip law A few days after a law has been enacted, it is officially published first as a slip law. Slip laws are unbound and printed on one or a few pages of paper.

standing committee Permanent committees established under the standing rules of the Senate or House and specializing in the consideration of particular subject areas.

United States *Statutes at Large* A chronological listing of the laws enacted each congressional section. They are published in volumes numbered by Congress.

veto The procedure established under the Constitution by which the president refuses to approve a bill or joint resolution and thus prevents its enactment into law. A regular veto occurs when the president returns the legislation to the chamber in which it originated. The President usually returns a vetoed bill with a message indicating his or her reasons for rejecting the measure. The veto can be overridden by a two-thirds vote in both the Senate and the House.

yield When a senator or representative who has been recognized to speak "yields" to another, he or she permits the other to speak but still retains the floor.

BIBLIOGRAPHY

Baker, Ross K. *House and Senate*. 3rd ed. New York: W.W. Norton, 2000.

Dove, Robert B. *Enactment of a Law*. Washington, D.C.: U.S. Government Printing Office, 2005.

Heineman, Robert A., Steven A. Peterson, and Thomas H. Rasmussen. *American Government*. 2nd ed. New York: McGraw-Hill, 1995.

Johnson, Charles W. *How Our Laws Are Made*. Washington, D.C.: U.S. Government Printing Office, 2003.

Koenig, Louis William. *Congress and the President: Official Makers of Public Policy*. Chicago: Scott Foresman, 1965.

McKay, David H. *Essentials of American Government*. Boulder, Colo.: Westview Press, 2000.

Want, Robert S. *How Federal Laws Are Made*. 3rd ed. Washington, D.C.: Want Pub, 1996.

FURTHER READING

Bernstein, Richard B., and Jerome Agel. *The Congress (Into the Third Century)*. New York: Walker, 1989.

Jordan, Terry L. *The U.S. Constitution: And Fascinating Facts About It*. Naperville, Ill.: Oak Hill, 1999.

Ragsdale, Bruce A. *The House of Representatives*. New York: Chelsea House, 1989.

Ritchie, Donald A. *The Congress of the United States: A Student Companion*. 2nd ed. New York: Oxford University Press, 2001.

———. *The Senate*. New York: Chelsea House, 1988.

Web Sites

The Library of Congress
http://www.loc.gov/index.html

U.S. Government Printing Office
http://www.gpo.gov/

U.S. House of Representatives
http://www.house.gov/

U.S. Senate
http://www.senate.gov/

PICTURE CREDITS

PAGE:

INDEX

ABOUT THE AUTHOR

BILL SCHEPPLER is an award-winning nonfiction author who has written on a broad array of subjects, from the Ironman Triathlon to the Mississippi Burning Trial of 1967. He has a keen interest in United States history and government. Scheppler, who holds a bachelors degree in history, currently writes and resides in the San Francisco Bay Area with his wife and their daughter.